D1140944

HANDBOOKS OF EUROPEAN NATIONAL DANCES

EDITED BY

VIOLET ALFORD

DANCES OF PORTUGAL

Plate 1
Ribatejo

DANCES of PORTUGAL

LUCILE ARMSTRONG

PUBLISHED
UNDER THE AUSPICES OF
THE ROYAL ACADEMY OF DANCING
AND THE
LING PHYSICAL EDUCATION ASSOCIATION

LONDON
MAX PARRISH & COMPANY

FIRST PUBLISHED IN 1948 BY
MAX PARRISH & CO LIMITED
51A RATHBONE PLACE LONDON W.1
IN ASSOCIATION WITH
ADPRINT LIMITED LONDON

ILLUSTRATED BY
LUCILE ARMSTRONG
MUSIC ARRANGED FOR THE PIANO BY
FERDINAND RAUTER

PRINTED IN GREAT BRITAIN
BY JARROLD & SONS LTD NORWICH
MUSIC PHOTO-SET BY
WOLFGANG PHILIPP ZURICH-HINTEREGG

CONTENTS

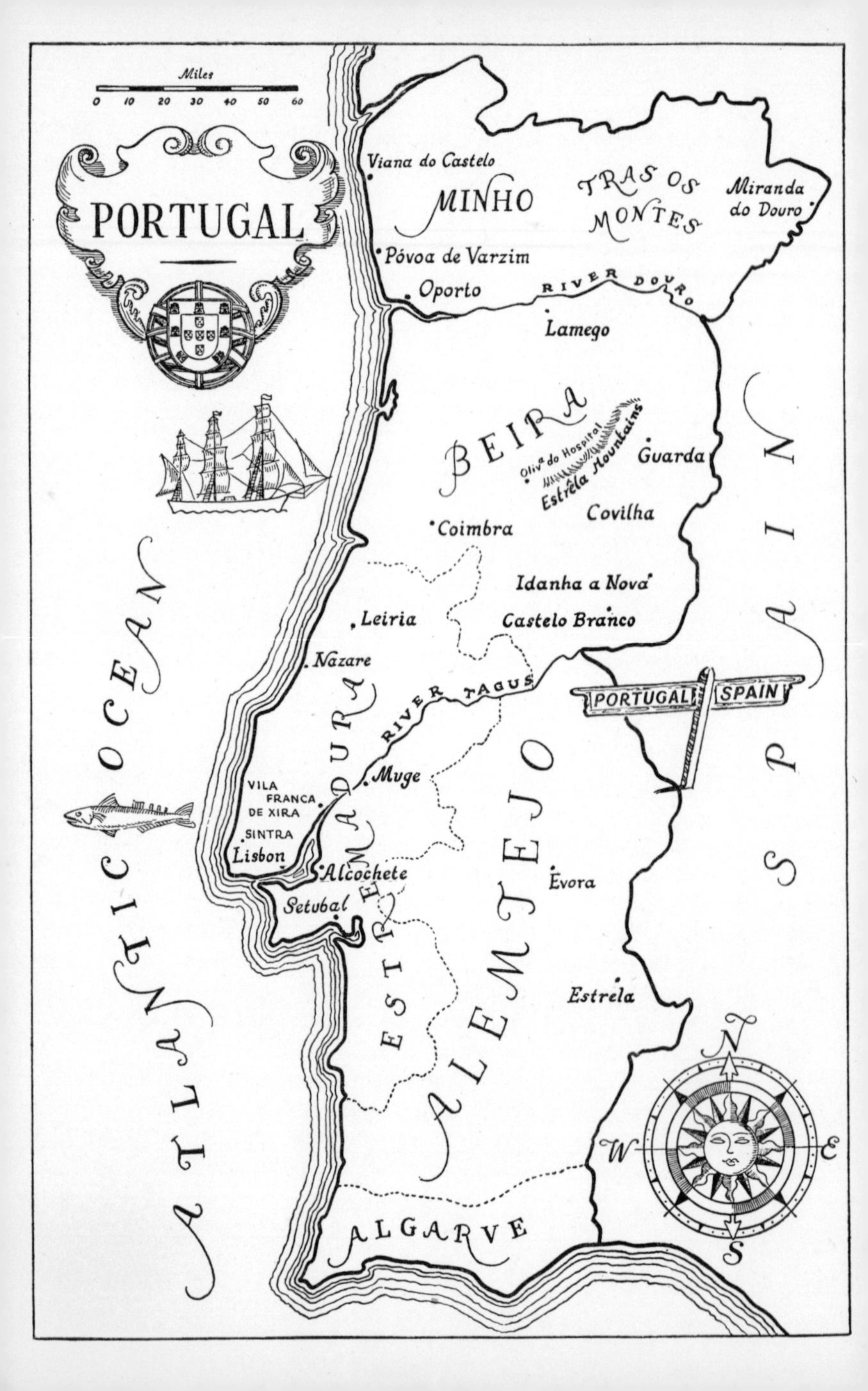

Miles
0 10 20 30 40 50 60
PORTUGAL
Viana do Castelo
MINHO
TRAS OS MONTES
Miranda do Douro
Póvoa de Varzim
Oporto
RIVER DOURO
Lamego
BEIRA
Oliva do Hospital
Estrêla Mountains
Guarda
Covilha
Coimbra
Idanha a Nova
Leiria
Castelo Branco
Nazare
RIVER TAGUS
PORTUGAL
SPAIN
ATLANTIC OCEAN
ESTREMADURA
Muge
VILA FRANCA DE XIRA
SINTRA
Lisbon
Alcochete
Setubal
ALEMTEJO
Évora
Estrela
ALGARVE
N
W
E
S

INTRODUCTION

PORTUGAL, allied to north-west Spain in the north, to Andalusian civilisation in the south, is as ethnically varied as her great neighbour. No single Portuguese dance or costume can represent the whole country, for each province has its own characteristics. In the northern province of Tras-os-Montes simple rhythms and figures are predominant, and the weather being cold in winter high jumps are included in their dances. As one goes south so the dance becomes smoother. The chief characteristic is a 3/4 or 6/8 step, sometimes as a Waltz step, sometimes as a Pas de Basque. Long dances are found chiefly along the northern coast, but the Round is the favourite.

Inland, along the northern Spanish frontier, lies the lovely Minho province. There time seems to have stood still for a couple of hundred years. In summer one can see good dances performed in the open air: the Minho Vira—different from the Lisbon Vira; the Gota of the Longways Country Dance type; the Pretinho, similar to the Gota but getting quicker and quicker, while the dance-song sings of the black King of the Monkeys; the Pai do Ladrão, a Round dance with a girl in the middle, her partner kneeling in front of her at a given line. There is also the Verdegaio (the Green Parrot), usually a Square for four, in many variants. The Chula too, which can be a Maia, a slow variant, the Passacalle which is a quick one. Chulas are generally longways with complicated figures and turns in the air. Near Oporto the men carry little sticks between the first and second, second and third fingers, clicking them like castanets. These sticks are called Chulas too, which is not a polite word, but the dancers do not mind that.

Solo dances, such as one sees in Andalusia, are non-existent, but the Fandango for one couple is one of the oldest dances in the Peninsula. In Alemtejo two men form the couple, or a man and a woman, facing each other and moving slightly in opposite directions. It is a competition or a challenge, each dancer showing off his steps in turn. When he is tired he waggles his feet from side to side while standing on his heels, the opponent then picks up the beat and shows what he can do. I once watched a couple hold the floor for forty-five minutes, neither of them repeating a step. The Fandango is found all over Spain and Portugal in varying forms, and in Portugal is sometimes danced in a longways formation by many couples vis-à-vis.

THE COAST

The most interesting dances are those of the fisherfolk along the coast and the banks of the Tagus. These people show a lively and intricate form, figures which sometimes look like the winding of coils of rope, apparently simple, but tricky and of an elusive rhythm which seems to denote an older tradition than the rest of Portugal can show. The music shows distinct Eastern influence—from the Moors one supposes. A village near Curia in the province of Beira Mar boasts a dance club, the Rancho das Cantarinhas. Cantarinhas are little jars, but these jars are far from little; they weigh about eight pounds when filled with sand and garlanded with flowers. The girls carry them on their heads during the complicated dance figures. No jars fall off, and no mistakes are made, in the smooth Waltz step faultlessly tapped out by their little *mules*.

The dances from Coimbra to Oporto along the coast are charmingly lively, for many couples and always accompanied by singing, not by instrumental music. This indeed applies to most of Portugal. Nazaré, another fishing town, possesses customs of its own. In summer a great feast takes place on the sands, in honour of Our Lady of Nazaré, lasting three days. After dancing on the sands for hours everyone lies down to sleep on them too.

In Povoa de Varzim the fisherfolk possess a capacity for high jumps and turns in the air, quite startling to see; the men wear a jersey of their own, embroidered in black and red, the designs of which are essentially maritime.

THE BEIRA PROVINCES

Further inland the little village of Paúl lies in the midst of mountains. Its simple, two-storeyed houses make an excellent background for the Round dances performed, as so often in this country, in the street. Here the whole village dances together, young and old, children and parents, and all are ready to take a turn in singing the accompaniment. The people of Paúl love singing in choirs. Sixty to eighty people will join in, which is remarkable for so small a community. Traditions are lively where the only access to a mountain fastness is by a rough road up which cars cannot go. The favourite type of dance seems to be a single line closing to a circle, all placing their arms over the shoulders of the persons on either side, moving first clockwise, then counter-clockwise, singing a traditional quatrain. Then the rhythm changes and all break into a Pas de Basque in 3/4 time. The Vira Corrido is danced here, but in a simpler form than further north towards Guarda, where it becomes a magnificent display of rapid turns and endurance.

East of Castelo Branco the village of Malpica owns a fine dance group, full of life. Their lovely costume with water-pleated skirts—the material wetted, pleated, and the pleats held in place by stones till dry—and chemises water-pleated also, and the hair plaited into a basket-shape, is, alas, rapidly falling into disuse. Here, Nature with her rolling country, rye fields and evergreen oaks, all clean and dry, makes for spotless cleanliness among the peasants. In the Estrèla mountains we find cold, huddled living conditions, people seeking warmth before cleanliness. The dances of Beira have much in common with each other, for they are variations of the fundamental triple step, used with raised arms and clicking fingers, and are chiefly in ring formation. With this recreational style we find a few ritual Maypole dances, chiefly towards the Spanish frontier.

ROUND LISBON

The Lisbon region is greatly spoilt from the dance point of view. The coast follows the fisherfolk type of dancing, inland is the Ribatejo (banks of the Tagus) type, and to the south of the capital one finds the Alemtejo type. The southern part of Portugal, like the southern part of Spain, is somewhat Moorish in character. The Moors remained there for many centuries and left their mark on customs, on place-names and on the race itself. Andalusian traditions, customs, men's costumes, and the very landscape seem to have crossed the frontier into Portuguese Alemtejo. This influence extends right up the Ribatejo with its breeding-farms for bulls and horses. The cowboys, called Campinos, wearing a picturesque costume smacking of Spain, live in dry heat in summer, and ride the interminable dusty roads, along which brightly painted mule-carts travel thirstily. Here riding is essential; the chief events of the year are the bull-fighting festivals and the fairs which take place in summer. The large ones attract the finest show of horses, the best dancing and the most attractive costumes.

The mounted Campinos are a joy to the eye, with their long lances and dignified air, but their dances are rather dull compared with those of fisherfolk of the same river region. The Campinos love the Round dance and the Fandango of Alemtejo already mentioned, which they perform remarkably well. In Muge, a village on the east of the Tagus, one can see the Campinos dancing the Fandango with a glass half-full of wine on their head and never spilling a drop, for all their antics.

These fisherfolk of the Ribatejo are excellent dancers. I asked to see dances at Vila Franca de Xira, and within ten minutes the room was full of people dancing the Real das Canas, the Cana being a reed which even if dropped on the ground will sprout and grow. In and out of the Tirana, the Vira de Oito, the Canaverde, the fisherfolk went, and it was always so beautifully done that an onlooker who had never seen them before exclaimed, 'I have been a ballet fan for years, but I have never seen anything so exquisite.' After all, a ballet can spring out of one man's inspiration, but it takes centuries to make a folk dance.

It is wonderful how many varieties of the 3/4 step come into being. The northern provinces rap out their rhythm with wooden clogs, or high-heeled *mules*. The Ribatejo women wear heavy shoes, so dances are simple with a good deal of marking time and stamping. The fisherwomen, on the other hand, accustomed to walking barefoot for miles on their rounds, also dance barefoot and have a magnificent carriage.

The Saloios of Lisbon and Estremadura are picturesque in their dull colours of stripes or check, the men wearing stocking caps or *barretes* of black or green, the women with their kerchiefs, each on a donkey taking farm produce to market. Many places round the capital now have forgotten all their dances, except the Vira. Round Cintra, a few villages still retain a few dances such as the Bailarico Saloio, the Verdegaio, the Canaverde. Sometimes one sees the Fandango of Alemtejo, but mostly the 'Fox' has taken their place, so that today only the older folk know the regional possessions. Among the wooded hills of Leiría they still dance Quadrilles and Schottisch, Viras of four or six, Vira Corrido, but here there is affinity with the dances of Beira, where arms are raised, fingers clicked, gaiety and laughter reign at a dance instead of the stiffly hanging arms and downcast eyes of the Lisbon region. The orange groves of Setúbal and the rich country round provide Round dances, and important feasts, such as at Cabo Espichel, Zezimbra, Alcácer Santiago de Cacem, give opportunities of seeing them to advantage.

THE ALEMTEJO

Only on rare occasions in the Alemtejo plains of grain and cork trees do people dance, for they live far apart and distances are great. Only at feasts such as sheep-shearing or Christmas do they meet, gathering together at the Montes (large farmhouses) to feast, sing and dance. Simple Round dances for as many couples as choose, arms waist-high and clicking fingers, are the rule, for tired legs, having walked for miles, are not inclined to jump. As one gets further south, arms are held lower and steps become shuffling. Some Spanish Alegrías rhythms have crossed this southern frontier and become indigenous. The poverty of the workmen is reflected in their poor dress, as compared with the northern costumes.

ALGARVE, THE FAR SOUTH

In Algarve, land of intense sun, the heat makes for fiery tempers and quick dance. The Corridinho is the regional dance, a circular type of Polka in pairs. Along the coast towards Spain, memories of the Moors prevail. For instance, in Pechai (Olhoa) there is a traditional Dança dos Mouros, Dance of the Moors, performed in September, probably a survival of one of the ceremonial Moriscas of the Peninsula, those dance-battles between Christians and Moors.

RITUAL DANCES

Portugal is as rich in seasonal ritual dances as any country in Europe, and possesses one of the best and fullest examples of that extraordinary medley, the Dance-drama of the Morisca type. At the village of Sobrado, not far from Oporto, Midsummer Day brings out the Moors and the *Bugios*, shows the ceremonial ploughing and sowing of a pre-Christian spring rite. In Miranda, Tras-os-Montes, a splendid example of a men's ritual Stick dance exists, the dancers in women's starched white petticoats, and all the 'Morris' paraphernalia of flowered hats, scarves and ribbons. This is an ornate performance of many figures. There is the Dance of King David at Braga, also on Midsummer Day, which perhaps was once as exciting a Morisca as that at Sobrado, but which evidently got into the hands of the priests and was renamed in biblical style. There is a Sword dance in Lisbon itself, the men piling up on each other's shoulders into a 'Castle'; there are ceremonial Maypole dances for men, and the curious Pinhata dances at Carnival round Lisbon, in which a huge pine cone opens, out of which pigeons fly and flowers fall. There are Giants and Dwarfs, Dragons and Mummers, too deeply embedded in the life of the people to be altogether omitted, but too anthropological a study for the purposes of this book.

MUSIC

Bagpipes, met with from Scotland to Spain, are a favourite instrument in Northern Minho and Tras-os-Montes. Bagpipers are seen as far south as Lisbon at annual fairs and Romerias (pilgrimages) round Cintra. Yet the bagpiper is more often a Spaniard than a Portuguese. The drum and bagpipes, or two drums and a small pipe (flageolet) are the most usual instruments in the Beiras. In hills and plains alike dances are accompanied by song. In the mountains of

St. Mamede, Lamègo and Estrèla, shepherds play on a little home-made pipe which serves to fill the gaps when singers are out of breath. In the district of Castelo Branco and around Idanha, many songs have curious endings in high falsetto. That old and primitive instrument, the panpipes, is still used by knife-grinders all over Portugal. They are of boxwood, made near Braga, or brought over the frontier from Galicia by the knife-grinders themselves, who are for the most part Galicians.

The Portuguese guitar is different from the Spanish one. It is pear-shaped, flat, has six double metal strings, and is played with the finger nail, or more usually with a piece of tortoiseshell. The Spanish guitar in Portugal is called *Viola* and is used only for accompaniments of songs or of the Portuguese guitar, while this last plays the tune and the *fioriture*. The Spanish habit of serenading a girl with a guitar is still continued in the south and along the Tagus, but chiefly in Coimbra. In this town it is done by the University students with Fados, but in other parts of the country a serenade will be more or less folk music. The Fado is the love-song of Coimbra, a peculiar form of plaintive melody and verse which requires special attention. For this two books are recommended in the Bibliography.

A most important instrument in the Peninsula is the drum. These are of all sorts and all sizes. Portugal has her varieties, the largest of which is the Zé Pereira. This is played on both faces and held in place by a cord round the player's neck. The Zé Pereiras roll out a deep and powerful note which carries for miles. It is intriguing that they should be called Joseph Peartree. Was the wooden frame once made of pear-tree wood? In the Estrèla mountains on the eve of Romérias or feasts, large goat-skin drums are beaten. These are the Bombos and as the name denotes, their deep sound booms across the hills to announce the feast. This is made more effective by the drummer knocking the Bombo smartly with his knee, thereby throwing it up in the air to shoulder level, pounding it all the time with his sticks to give out a thunderous roll.

South of Covilhâ (Estrèla) and near Portalegre on the Spanish frontier, a square hand-drum or tambourine is used —the Adufe. About fifteen inches square, it is held diagonally, but upright, between the hands, so the rhythm can be drummed out with the fingers of both hands. An incredible number of rhythms can be got from this, and these, coupled with the different tones according to which fingers are used, carry one away to the Caucasus and the East where similar rhythms are heard. The square drum was well known in Spain up to some fifty years ago, where it was painted with elaborate figures—often sacred ones—and had ribbons at the corners. In Portugal it is sometimes painted too, while inside it has pieces of tin to make a tambourine-like sound and sympathetic strings inside to increase the resonance.

COSTUME

Footgear. The Minho province has plenty of trees to provide wooden soles. Women wear high, leather boots with wooden soles to work in the fields, go barefoot with their lovely gait in summer, or use wooden-soled *mules*. Fisherfolk use wooden soles for everyday, but on feast days all the women wear dainty leather or velvet *mules* exquisitely embroidered in sequins, or in coloured wools and thread about Viana do Castelo. The tap of high-heeled *mules* is a feature of Minho dances. Heavier footwear is needed in mountain districts, whereby dance steps tend to become simplified as in the North-East. Among the cowboy riders of the Tagus district dances are held on threshing-floors of beaten earth, where they wear leather shoes, and the stepping has deteriorated in consequence. Stamping is characteristic of these Campinos, their style strongly contrasting with that of the barefoot fisherfolk.

Headwear. The kerchief is an important part of costume. The very fact of wearing it makes the wearer hold up her head, while carrying jars and other burdens on the head gives a beautiful carriage. There are many ways of wearing the kerchief—knotted under the chin, folded so that three ends are on the top of the head, crossed under the chin and brought round to be tied at the back of the head, crossed under the chin and the ends well tucked in, or simply hanging down at the back from the top of the head. Each way has its own charm.

Dress. The show costume of Portugal is that of Minho. It is worn only in the villages round Viana do Castelo and in a few over the Spanish Galician frontier. The so-called Lavradeira consists of a homespun striped linen skirt, the general effect being splashes of red. The dress is made at home by its wearer, so each differs slightly from the next. Skirts have a broad band of red or black according to the village; some are embroidered in bright wools and sequins. Aprons are so thickly woven with multi-coloured flowers that they feel like carpets. On the waist-gathers a word is embroidered—'Amor' or 'Maria', or the place, 'Viana'. The chemise is linen, embroidered at neck and cuffs and on the shoulders. Tradition demands floral designs in blue. The bodice is always of two colours, red above, black below, but a pale purple, wine, pale blue or olive green may be substituted. Back and front are generously embroidered like the skirt, with wool and sequins. A bright-red kerchief with contrasting woven roses and fringes is often worn over the shoulders, and crossed over the breast. The colour of head and shoulder kerchief changes in each village. This is called the Red dress. The Blue dress is similar in cut, chiefly black except for the apron with coloured flowers, but the kerchief must have a dark-blue or purple ground.

Stockings for both costumes are knitted in open lacy patterns in white thread. As much gold as possible is worn, chains round the neck, gold filigree hearts, crosses and ear-rings to match. The hanging pocket is a veritable jewel of miniature embroidery.

Minho brides wear black or very dark blue velvet or cloth embroidered in jet, but any funereal aspect is dissipated by gold braid on skirt and apron, and by a fine white lace kerchief over the head. Bridegrooms appear in light-grey suits or respectable black.

The men's costume round Viana and Braga is usually black or dark blue with velvet waistcoat to match. The jacket is lined with red flannel, trimmed with solid silver buttons down the front and on the cuffs, sewn on in a curve.

Vila Franca de Xira (Tagus district) has its Campinos dress. The girl in Plate 1 wears stiff white petticoats, and probably a red flannel one as well, over her linen chemise. On Sundays a white blouse is preferred. The short apron may be of any colour; bright colours for the headkerchief which may be tied at the nape of the neck, under the chin, or on the top of the head. In winter a huge, dull-coloured shawl serves as a cloak. As many gold chains as possible are worn round the neck.

The Campino wears tight-fitting dark breeches, a white shirt, sometimes frilled, and a double-breasted, scarlet-fronted flannel waistcoat, with the monogram of the proprietor for whom he works embroidered on the left side. It is he who wears the *Barrete Verde*, the green stocking-cap, which gives its name to the famous festival at Alcochete. When not dancing he carries over his left shoulder a black, or very dark-blue, short jacket of Andalusian cut. This costume is kept for feast days and will only be seen on those occasions. To protect him from the rain which sweeps in from the Atlantic, he wears the split-up sheepskin apron and long-tailed jacket of Alemteio, or a modern version of the travelling cape of about 1800, called *Capa Alemtejana*. His masters, the landed proprietors of this riverine district, wear the Spanish Andalusian costume of short jacket, tight-fitting trousers and wide Cordoban hat.

The girls in and around Coimbra, known as Tricanas, wear a sober costume. The distinguishing mark of the Tricana is the large blanket-shawl worn in a manner peculiar to the district. A scarlet kerchief sometimes brightens the effect, and the elegant patent-leather *mules* bear a design in white thread. In Coimbra itself they wear a black headkerchief gathered on a thread round the back of the neck, and a black velvet ribbon under the chin, with a quite seductive effect. The man's costume is seldom seen round Coimbra, though further north it is fairly common: double-breasted waistcoat edged with black braid and lined with red flannel, tight-fitting cloth trousers, wide at the bottom; in summer the striped cotton suit without a tie, but with an embroidered shirt.

Skirts. Fisherwomen and peasant women wear very wide skirts, and their dances seem to have developed into Viras (which means turns) in order to show off the top-like skirt in the constant spins of the dance. In the Tagus Ribatejo district where skirts are not so wide, the dancers rely on stamping and figures for their effects, rather than on turns, while again towards Castelo Branco the thick woollen and pleated skirts engender an endless succession of turns in the dances. The coastal districts of Minho are also noted for wide skirts and turns, of which the Vira Corrido is full, the top couple working its way down the lines of dancers who stand vis-à-vis, turning perpetually to right and left, skirts billowing wide with a lovely spinning effect.

Plates 2
Minho

SOME FESTIVALS WHERE DANCING MAY BE SEEN

Ascension Day	Evora and many places. Picking wheat-ears and poppies. Pilgrimage dances.
Corpus Christi Day	Many places. Processions with giants, dwarfs, guilds, dances.
Midsummer	June 24th. Figuera da Foz. Fishermen's and peasant dances. June 24th. Braga. Dance of King David. June 24th. Sobrado (Valongo). Mouriscada, a Dance-Drama. June 24th. Cintra. Dances and processions. June 24th. Lisbon. Dances and processions.
July	Vila Franca de Xira. Date announced in papers. Bulls running through streets. Dances by cowboys and fishermen. Festa do Colete Encarnado.
July 6th	Guimarães. Procession of St. Torquate. Offerings, dances.
August	Villages round Cintra. Decorated carts, dances, Festa do Cirio.
August	Santarem. Date announced in papers. Bull-fighting festival (Portuguese style). Dances.
August 15th and September 14th	Póvoa de Varzim. Fishermen's Feast. Mass on the beach. Dances.
Third Sunday in August	Viana (Minho). Nossa Senhora da Agonía. Procession, dances, exhibition of costumes, fair.

Last Sunday in August	Miranda de Douro and other villages. Dança dos Paulitos, men's ritual dance.
September 2nd	Viana. Harvest offerings. Giants; dwarfs; dances.
September	Alcochete (Ribatejo). Date announced in papers. Festa do Barrete Verde. Bulls, dances, fair.
September 16th	Ericeira. Fishermen's procession of offerings. Dances.

St. John the Baptist's Eve and Day (Midsummer), St. Anthony, St. Peter and Carnival, especially the Sunday, Monday and Tuesday before Lent, are also excellent occasions for seeing dances and celebrations.

SOME GROUPS THAT PRACTISE THEIR REGIONAL DANCES

Grupo Folklorico de Entre-Douro e Minho (in Lisbon).

Grupo Folklorico de Bailaricos. Cintra.

Grupo Folklorico de Nazaré. Estremadura.

Esticadinhos de Cantanhede. Beira Mar.

Grupo Folklorico de São João da Madeira. Beira Mar.

Grupo Folklorico de Póvoa de Varzim (near Oporto).

Grupo Folklorico de Carreço. Viana do Castelo.

Grupo Folklorico de Sta. Marta de Portugelo, Viana do Castelo.

Grupo Folklorico de Mealhada. Beira Mar.

THE DANCES

TECHNICAL EDITOR, MURIEL WEBSTER
ASSISTED BY KATHLEEN P. TUCK

ABBREVIATIONS
USED IN DESCRIPTION OF THE STEPS AND DANCES

r—right } referring to
l—left } hand, foot etc.
C—clockwise

R—right } describing turns or
L—left } ground pattern
C-C—counter-clockwise

For descriptions of foot positions and explanations of any ballet terms the following books are suggested for reference:

A Primer of Classical Ballet (Cecchetti method). Cyril Beaumont.

First Steps. Ruth French and Felix Demery.

The Ballet Lover's Pocket Book. Kay Ambrose.

REFERENCE BOOKS FOR DESCRIPTION OF FIGURES:

The Scottish Country Dance Society's Publications. Many volumes, from Thornhill, Cairnmuir Road, Edinburgh 12.

The English Folk Dance and Song Society's Publications. Cecil Sharp House, 2 Regent's Park Road, London N.W.1.

The Country Dance Book I–VI. Cecil J. Sharp. Novello & Co., London.

POISE OF THE BODY AND CHARACTERISTIC ARM GESTURES

In the North—Tras-os-Montes, Minho and the Beiras—the peasants hold their heads well poised and their arms high (see Plate 4).

In the South, the arms are held lower, in Alemtejo the girls' arms being only waist-high when not held on partners' hips or shoulders.

In Lisbon, where modern influence has crept in, arms are also held low, and the general poise of the body is less good than in the country where the traditional poise of body and head has been maintained.

Tagus fishermen hold themselves proudly like the Northerners, although their arms are held low, just above those of the girl, which are about waist height.

BASIC STEPS

Running step (as in A Rosa).

2 light runs to each bar, the body weight slightly back and the feet slightly forward.

Polka step (as in Padeirinha).

This is more correctly a hop change of step in which the feet do not close up.

		MUSIC *Beats*
1	Hop on l, swing r forward.	and
2	Step forward r.	1
3	Step forward l.	and
4	Step forward r.	2
	Repeat beginning with hop on r.	

Pas de Basque

This name is used for facility of reference although the basic Pas de Basque of the ballet is never used. The step varies according to the music.

A. 6/8 time.

The characteristic of this variation is the marked circling of the leg (rond-de-jambe) to start the movement and the slight turn of the body from side to side.

		MUSIC *Beats*
1	Circle r leg, turning on ball of l to face R.	and
2	Step on r, swinging l leg across r on the ground.	1
3	Step on l in front of r with momentary transfer of weight.	and
4	Step on r behind l, preparing to circle l leg in order to repeat the step turning to L on ball of r foot.	2

B. 3/4 time, as in many Viras.

Start with l and travel forward on each Pas de Basque.

1	Circle l leg (rond-de-jambe) taking weight on to it in 3rd position behind (coupé under).	and 1
2	Step forward r.	2
3	Close l to r in 3rd position behind.	3

Repeat beginning with circling of the r leg. This step is danced on the balls of the feet with very little spring.

C. 2/4 time.

This step is similar to A, but the turn to R and L is 90° instead of about 45°. The whole movement is big and very flat, the accent again being on the circling of the leg at the beginning of the step. Count "and 1 and 2".

D. The time signature varies according to the region. In the East it is generally 2/4 but otherwise 6/8. The footwork is more like the Scottish pas de basque, but in the Vira the step is generally used with a turn. In the East this step changes to a step hop or high skip.

E. As in Vira Extrapassado.

This step might best be described as a spring Waltz.

1	Spring on to r.	1
2	Step forward on l.	2
3	Step forward on r.	3

The men change the step completely as the dance works up.

1	Step forward r.	1 2
2	Hop on r, bring l knee forward.	3

A ROSA (To Rose)

Region Oliveira do Hospital, Beira. Plates 3 and 4.

Character Quick light movement of feet.

Formation Round dance for as many couples as will; partners facing each other—men C-C, women C—to form a single ring.

Dance A light running step is used throughout (2 steps to each bar); the arms are curved slightly, and are moved about six inches from right to left just above shoulder level, the fingers clicking on every beat. This arm and finger movement is continued throughout the dance.

	MUSIC *Bars*
FIGURE I	
1 All move C with 8 running steps starting with inside foot, the men travelling backward and the women forward.	A 1–4
2 Repeat to place, the men forward and the women backward.	1–4
FIGURE II	
1 4 running steps turning inward away from own partner, advancing to meet the man or woman behind; 4 running steps turning inward advancing to meet own partner.	B 1–4
Repeat.	1–4
FIGURE III	
1 Partners turn each other C with 8 running steps—r hand on partner's l hip, l hand holding partner's r hand on own hip. Partners pull slightly away and look at one another.	C 1–4
2 As 1, turning C-C with opposite arm round partner.	5–8
Repeat the whole dance twice finishing with figure 1, so that music A is played for the third time.	

A ROSA

From Oliveira do Hospital, Beira
Noted by Lucile Armstrong

Allegretto **A** *Dance. Last time quicker*

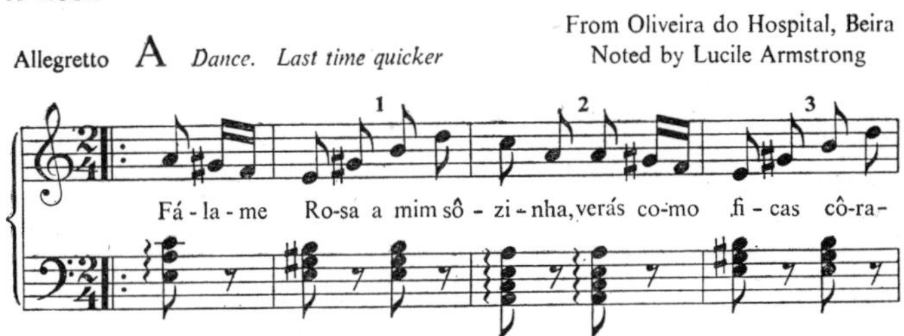

The sequence A, A, B, B, C *is played 3 times. After the last* C *play* A, A *to finish.*

PADEIRINHA (*Little Baker Girl*)

Regions	Vila Franca de Xira, Ribatejo. Plate 1. Beiras —various versions, this one from the plains of the Tagus danced by the Campinos.
Character	Clearly defined rhythms during the stamping movement.
Formation	Round for as many couples as desired, to form a double ring with the women on the inside.
Dance	Throughout the dance couples hold hands crossed behind backs.

	MUSIC *Bars*
FIGURE I	A
1 6 Polka steps travelling C-C.	1–6
2 Repeat 1.	1–6
FIGURE II	
1 3 Polka steps turning C on spot, partners looking at one another, 5 stamps, l, r, l, r, l, in rhythm of quick, quick, quick, slow, slow.	B 1–4
2 3 Polka steps turning C-C on spot, finishing with 5 stamps as before.	5–8
Repeat Figure II.	1–8
Repeat the whole dance 3 times or more.	

PADEIRINHA

From Vila Franca de Xira, Ribatejo
Noted by Lucile Armstrong

Play whole dance 3 times or more

Nem à fonte, nem ao rio
Não foi capaz de te vêre.
Óra báte Padeirinha saiba pôr o pé na areia,
Óra báte Padeirinha teu amôr 'sta na cadeia.

Plate 3 *Coimbra*

Bussaco

Plate 4

VIRA EXTRAPASSADO (Progressive Turning Dance)

Region Santa Marta, Viana, Minho. Plate 2.

Character The dance is marked by the gradual increase and decrease in movement. The step is worked up from a slight swaying motion, which the dancers use when waiting to be turned, to a smooth Waltz step or Pas de Basque (see *Basic Steps*, E) which the women maintain throughout, and to a high step hop which the men use when all the dancers are in action. This step dies down as gradually fewer couples are turning, and the dance finishes with the swaying motion as at the beginning.

Formation Longways for as many as will—couples face each other, the men and women standing alternately. See diagram (○ = woman, □ = man).

1	2	3	4
○	□	○	□
□	○	□	○
1	2	3	4

Dance Two smooth Waltz or Pas de Basque steps are used for each arming, start with l foot.

FIGURE	MUSIC *Bars*
	A
1 Top man turns partner with r arm once and a half to finish so that 1st man faces 2nd woman and 1st woman faces 2nd man.	1–2

VIRA EXTRAPASSADO

Noted by Lucile Armstrong
at Santa Marta, Viana, Minho

Quick Waltz time

Play A A, B B *continuously till all are in their original places.*

2	Turn 2nd couple with l arm to face partner.	3–4
3	Turn partners with r arm once round to face 3rd couple, so that 1st man faces 3rd woman and 1st woman faces 3rd man.	5–6
4	Turn 3rd couple with l arm to face partner.	7–8
	Continue as above, a new top couple now starting simultaneously with the original top couple.	
1	Turn partner with r arm to finish facing couple below.	9–10
2	Turn couple below with l arm.	11–12
3	Turn partners with r arm.	13–14
4	Turn couple below with l arm.	15–16
	As the original top couple gets to the bottom they gradually work up the set until all couples return to place. The couple being turned must always finish in the place of the couple above them so that the set does not move down the floor.	
	N.B.—Men must always turn women and vice versa. When turning partners couples make alternately a turn and a half and one turn because of the men and women being on alternate sides. At the end of the whole dance the men offer inside hands to partners and lead them off.	

Note.—The dance is very similar to Strip the Willow (Scottish Country Dance) which is danced to a running step in 9/8 rhythm and in which a new couple does not start until the original 1st couple has reached the bottom.

VIRA (*one of the many variations*)

Region — Lisbon region. No special costume is given for this Vira as it is often danced by townsfolk in ordinary modern dress.

Character — Smooth at first, breaking into gay skipping in the second step.

Formation — Dance for two couples in a circular formation. All have left shoulders towards the centre of the set, partners diagonally opposite one another as in diagram:

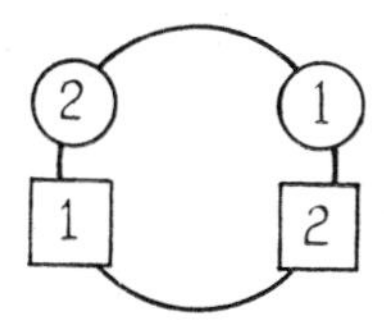

Dance — Throughout this dance the arms are held as in A Rosa, hands about one foot apart. Fingers are clicked on the first beat of every bar. The body is inclined slightly backward and partners look at each other throughout the dance.

		MUSIC *Bars*
		A
I	16 Pas de Basque (see *Basic Steps*, B) travelling C-C, beginning with l foot. Body sways alternately to L and R towards the side of the foot that goes behind.	I–8 re- peated

	B
2 Repeat 1, only dancing 15 Pas de Basque.	1–8 for repeat 1–7
At any time during music B and C a dancer may turn and dance backwards. Sometimes all the dancers turn R about on every 8th bar.	
3 During music C (16 bars) both couples dance simultaneously, but for facility of description the sequence of movement of each couple is described separately:	C
No. 1 couple—l shoulders towards centre of set.	
Skip forward on l foot towards partners beginning to turn L.	1
Skip forward on r foot with a stamp, completing a half-turn to L to face partner (open line).	2
Skip backward on l foot beginning to turn R.	3
Skip backward on r foot to finish with l shoulder towards centre	4
4 skips to change places with partners, travelling C-C and making $1\frac{1}{2}$ turns to L to finish with l shoulder to centre.	5–8
	C
Repeat, partners finishing in original places.	1–8

Note.—When B is played and danced the second time, bar 8 is omitted, and the syllable "Ó" is actually sung on the last beat of bar 7.

The sequence AA, BB, CC is repeated three times or more.

VIRA (Lisbon region)
Allegretto Smooth Waltz time
A
Noted by Lucile Armstrong
Me – ni – nas va-mos ao Vi – ra, Ai, que o Vi – ra
é coi – sa bo – a
(1st). Me-
(2nd) Eu
B
já vi dan-çar o
Vi – ra, Ai, as me – ni – nas de Lis – bo – a
(1st) Eu
(2nd) Ó
C
Faster
Vi – ra, ó Vi – ra, ó Vi – ra vi – rou, As
vol-tas do Vi – ra sou Eu que as dou. Ó
dou
C (2nd time). Ó Vira, ó Vira, ó Vira virei, As voltas do Vira sou Eu que as dei.

No. 2 couple—l shoulders to centre.	C
Balance to L and R.	1–2
They then pick up the sequence as danced by couple No. 1.	
Skip forward on l foot, skip forward on r with stamp.	3–4
Skip backward on l foot, skip backward on r.	5–6
4 skips to cross over into partner's place.	7–8
Skip forward on l foot, skip forward on r	1–2
with stamp.	3–4
Skip backward on l foot, skip backward on r.	5–6
4 skips to cross to original places.	7–8
N.B.—the last 2 skips will be danced to music A as couple No. 2 starts the skips 2 bars later than couple No. 1.	A 1–2
Repeat the dance 3 times or more.	

NOTE

We beg you not to think of Regional costumes as fancy dress. They are held in honour by their wearers as an important part of their heritage. Respect them. Do not dress dancers in a make-believe Spanish costume to dance A Rosa. You would be equally justified in dressing a Helston Furry dancer in a Highland kilt.

The Editor

BIBLIOGRAPHY

ALFORD, VIOLET. 'Morris and Midsummer in Portugal.' *Folk-Lore*, vol. XLIV, June, 1933.

ALFORD, VIOLET, and RODNEY GALLOP.—*The Traditional Dance*. London, 1935.

BASTO, CLAUDIO.—*O Trajo a Vianèsa*. Gaia, 1930. (The Viana Costume.)

BASTO, CLAUDIO.—*Turcos e Cristãos*. Batalha em Ribeira-Pontede (Turks and Christians.)

CARDOSO, MARTA.—*A Dança em Portugal*. Porto. (The Dance in Portugal.)

GALLOP, RODNEY.—*Portugal*. Cambridge University Press, 1936. (Customs, Dances, Fado, Songs.)

GOLDING, E.—'The Fado,' in *Anglo-Portuguese News* during 1943.

PIMENTEL, ALBERTO.—*A Dança em Portugal*. Porto. (The Dance in Portugal.)

TOMÁS, P. DE FERNÁNDES.—*Canções Populares da Beira*. Porto. (Folk Songs from Beira.)

VASCONCÈLOS, L. DE.—*Ensaios Etnográficos*. Tradições Populares do Portugal, vols. I–VI. (Ethnographical Studies. Popular Traditions of Portugal.)

Note.—There is an extreme scarcity of notated Portuguese dances in published form.